𝒜 Poem makes us see

everything   for the first time

todo   por primera vez

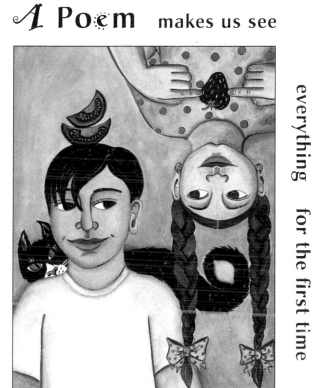

Un poema nos hace ver

a mis sobrinitos Itzy, Tony, Sammy e Isabelle, con mucho cariño —F.X.A.

To Mona, Maui, Boris, Ra, and especially Liza —M.C.G.

Francisco X. Alarcón is an award-winning Chicano poet. The author of
seven books of poetry and the co-author of several textbooks for Spanish speakers,
he is Director of the Spanish for Native Speakers Program at the University of California, Davis.

Maya Christina Gonzalez is a painter and graphic artist. Her first
picture book for Children's Book Press, *Prietita and the Ghost Woman* by
Gloria Anzaldúa, was highly praised for its magnificent imagery. She lives in San Francisco, California.

Poems copyright © 1997 by Francisco X. Alarcón. All rights reserved.   Pictures copyright © 1997 by Maya Christina Gonzalez. All rights reserved.

Editor: Harriet Rohmer   *Design and Production:* Cathleen O'Brien   *Editorial/Production Assistant:* Laura Atkins

Thanks to the staff of Children's Book Press: Andrea Durham, Janet Levin, Emily Romero, Stephanie Sloan, and Christina Tarango.

Library of Congress Cataloging-in-Publication Data
Alarcón, Francisco X, 1954–
Laughing tomatoes and other spring poems = Jitomates Risueños y otros poemas de primavera:
poems by Francisc X. Alarcón; pictures by Maya Christina Gonzalez.   p.   cm.   Text in English and Spanish.
Summary: A bilingual collection of humoros and serious poems about family, nature, and celebrations by a renowned Mexican American poet.
ISBN 0-89239-199-5 (paperback) 1. Children's poetry, American. 2. Spring—Juvenile poetry. 3. American poetry—Mexican American authors. 4. Children's poetry,
American—Translations into Spanish. 5. Children's poetry, Hispanic American (Spanish)—Translations into English. [1. Spring—Poetry. 2. Nature—Poetry. 3. American
poetry—Mexican American authors. 4. Mexican American poetry (Spanish). 5. Spanish language materials—Bilingual.]
1. Gonzalez, Maya Christina, ill. II. Title   PS3551.L22L38   1997   811'.54-dc20   96-7459   CIP   AC

Printed in Singapore by Tien Wah Press
10 9 8 7 6 5 4 3 2 1

Children's Book Press is a nonprofit publisher of multicultural and bilingual literature for children, supported in part by grants from the California Arts Council.
Write us for a complimentary catalog: Children's Book Press, 2211 Mission Street, San Francisco, CA 94110.
Visit our website: www.childrensbookpress.org

Distributed to the book trade by Publishers Group West
Quantity discounts available through the publisher for educational and nonprofit use.

Laughing Tomatoes

and Other Spring Poems

Jitomates Risueños

y otros poemas de primavera

Poems/Poemas 🍅 Francisco X. Alarcón

Illustrations/Ilustraciones 🍅 Maya Christina Gonzalez

Children's Book Press/Libros para niños
San Francisco, California

Dew

the fresh
taste
of the night

El rocío

el fresco
sabor
de la noche

4

Roots

I carry
my roots
with me
all the time
rolled up
I use them
as my pillow

Raíces

mis raíces
las cargo
siempre
conmigo
enrolladas
me sirven
de almohada

5

Morning Sun

warming up
my bed
in the morning

the Sun
calls me
through the window

"wake up
get up
come on out"

Sol matutino

calentando
mi cama
en la mañana

el Sol
me llama
por la ventana

"despierta
levántate
ven afuera"

6

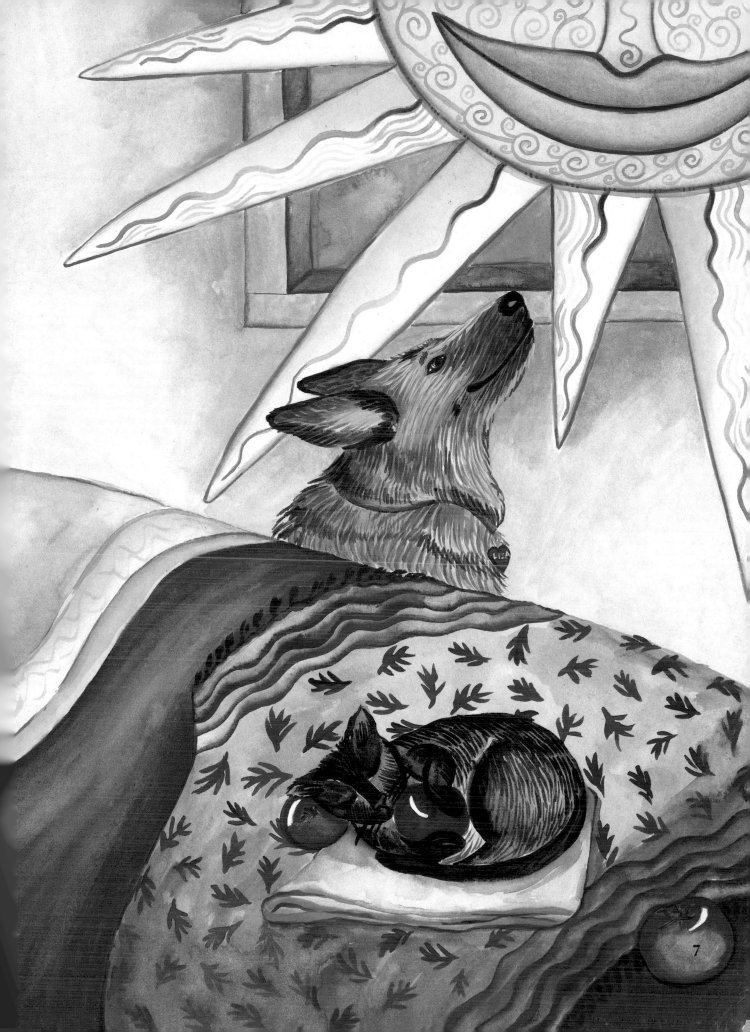

Las canciones de mi abuela

compartían
el ritmo
de la lavadora

transformaban
la cocina
en una pista de baile

consolaban
las sillas
patas arriba

alegraban
los retratos colgados
de la familia

arrullaban
las sábanas
en el tendedero

les daban sabor
a los frijoles
de olla

las canciones
que cantaba
mi abuela

eran capaces
de hacer salir
a las estrellas

convertir
a mi abuela
en una joven

que de nuevo
iba por agua
al río

y hacerla
reír y llorar
a la vez

My Grandma's Songs

would follow
the beat of
the washing machine

turning
our kitchen
into a dance floor

consoling
the chairs placed
upside down

delighting
the family portraits
on the walls

putting to sleep
the sheets
on the clothesline

giving flavor
to the boiling pot
of beans

the songs
my grandma
used to sing

could make
the stars
come out

could turn
my grandma
into a young girl

going back
to the river
for water

and make her
laugh and cry
at the same time

First Rain

is it raining
or
is the sky
crying?

Primera lluvia

¿llueve
o
llora
el cielo?

Flowers
the best
poems
around

Las flores
los mejores
poemas
a la redonda

Spring

the hills
are starting
to crack
a green smile
once again

Primavera

las colinas
comienzan
a sonreír
muy verdes
otra vez

11

Jitomates risueños

en el jardín
plantamos
jitomates

los vegetales
más felices
de todos

alegres
se redondean
de sabor

risueños
se ponen
colorados

convirtiendo
sus arbustos
alambrados

en árboles
de Navidad
en primavera

Laughing Tomatoes

in our backyard
we plant
tomatoes

the happiest
of all
vegetables

with joy
they grow round
with flavor

laughing
they change
to red

turning
their wire-framed
bushes

into
Christmas trees
in spring

Oda al maíz

padre
madre
regalo
del sol

tierra
agua
aire
luz

como
las razas
del mundo
te apareces

negro
amarillo
rojo
y blanco

tus elotes
nacen
apuntando
al cielo

tu pelo
de seda
lo mece
el viento

hermana
hermano
venado
verde

mis manos
cosecharán
tus sonrisas
enmascaradas

Ode to Corn

father
mother
gift from
the sun

earth
water
air
light

like
the races
of the world
you appear

black
yellow
red
and white

your tender ears
are born
pointing
to the sky

the wind
caresses
your silky
hair

sister
brother
green
deer

my hands
will harvest
your veiled
big smiles

Tortilla

each tortilla
is a tasty
round of applause
for the sun

La tortilla

cada tortilla
es una sabrosa
ronda de aplausos
para el sol

16

Chile

sometimes
a bite is all it takes
for a supernova
to explode

El chile

a veces basta
una mordida
para que explote
una supernova

Cinco de Mayo

una batalla
en los libros
de historia

una fiesta
de música
y colores

una ocasión
para agitar
banderas

un baile
con piropos
y piñata

orchata
tostaditas
y guacamole

un mango
con chile
y limón

un grito
de alegría
y primavera

¡sí, ya mero
salimos
de vacaciones!

Cinco de Mayo celebra una victoria de patriotas mexicanos contra un ejército francés invasor en Puebla, México, el cinco de mayo de 1862.

Orchata es una sabrosa bebida de arroz.

Cinco de Mayo

a battle
in some
history books

a *fiesta*
of music
and colors

a flag
waving
occasion

a flirting
dance
and a *piñata*

orchata
corn chips
and *guacamole*

a mango
with some *chile*
and lemon

a cry
of joy
and spring

yes, summer
vacation is just
around the corner!

Cinco de Mayo is a holiday celebrating a victory of Mexican patriots over an invading French army in Puebla, Mexico, the fifth of May, in 1862.

Orchata is a tasty rice drink.

Las palabras son pájaros

las palabras
son pájaros
que llegan
con los libros
y la primavera

a las palabras
les gustan
las nubes
el viento
los árboles

hay palabras
mensajeras
que vienen
de muy lejos
de otras tierras

para éstas
no existen
fronteras
sino estrellas
luna y sol

hay palabras
familiares
como canarios
y exóticas
como el quetzal

unas resisten
el frío
otras se van
con el sol
hacia el sur

hay palabras
que se mueren
enjauladas
difíciles
de traducir

y otras
hacen nido
tienen crías
les dan calor
alimento

les enseñan
a volar
y un día
se marchan
en parvadas

las letras
en la página
son las huellas
que dejan
junto al mar

PEACE

Words are Birds

words
are birds
that arrive
with books
and spring

they
love
clouds
the wind
and trees

some words
are messengers
that come
from far away
from distant lands

for them
there are
no borders
only stars
moon and sun

some words
are familiar
like canaries
others are exotic
like the quetzal bird

some can stand
the cold
others migrate
with the sun
to the south

some words
die
caged—
they're difficult
to translate

and others
build nests
have chicks
warm them
feed them

teach them
how to fly
and one day
they go away
in flocks

the letters
on this page
are the prints
they leave
by the sea

PAZ

Strawberries

sweet
tender
hearts

oh! left by children
working
the fields

Las fresas

dulces
tiernos
corazones

¡ay! de niños
pizcando
el campo

Un árbol para César Chávez

A Tree for César Chávez

un roble
plantamos
en tu día

un roble
en medio
del parque

un roble
cada vez
más frondoso

un roble
con tus facciones
y tu espíritu

un roble
con los brazos
abiertos

un roble
para grandes
y chicos

un roble
listo para celebrar
tu cumpleaños

cada 31 de marzo
con hojas tiernas
de primavera

César Chávez (1927-1993) *Líder méxico-americano, fundador de un sindicato para los trabajadores del campo.*

an oak
we planted
on your day

an oak
in the middle
of the park

an oak
more bountiful
with time

an oak
with your features
and your spirit

an oak
with open
arms

an oak
for grown-ups
and children

an oak
ready to celebrate
your birthday

every March 31st
with tender leaves
of spring

César Chávez (1927-1993) *Mexican-American leader, founder of the United Farm Workers of America (UFWA).*

Sueño

soñé que había
un jardín
en cada casa

en las ventanas
de las oficinas
crecían jitomates

la gente
se saludaba
con flores

no había escuela
o iglesia
sin su jardín

todos tenían
buena mano
para plantar

y los coches
eran algo
del pasado

26

Dream

I dreamed
a garden
in every home

tomatoes
grew in
office windows

people greeted
each other
with flowers

no school
or church was
without a garden

everybody
had a green
thumb

and cars
were a thing
of the past

Other Voices

can you hear
the voices
between
these lines?

Otras voces

¿escuchas
las voces
entre
estas líneas?

28

Prayer of the Fallen Tree

brothers
and sisters
come swiftly

make me
part of
your nests

turn me
into an egg
a wing

I want
to fly
far away

be a seedling
in another
forest

Plegaria del árbol caído

hermanos
y hermanas
vengan rápido

háganme
parte
de sus nidos

conviértanme
en un huevo
un ala

quiero
volar
muy lejos

ser retoño
en algún
otro bosque

Afterword

A collection of poetry is like a tomato plant. From a small seed it sprouts, then grows and grows. Poems need good soil, sunlight, water, air, and lots of care and tending. Some of these poems were written first in Spanish, others in English, and some came out in both languages almost at the same time. Poems, like tomatoes, grow in many forms and shapes. And somehow they change every time you read them. This is the magic of poetry.

I started writing poems by jotting down the songs my grandma used to sing to us. I would write at the kitchen table, surrounded by our pets, smelling my grandma's delicious cooking. For me, poetry is about life, family, community. I also believe poems are really incomplete until someone reads them. Then they come alive and start dancing in the imagination. Yes, make these poems yours, as artist Maya Christina Gonzalez has made them hers. I want them to belong to you as much as they belong to us.

—*Francisco X. Alarcón*

Posdata

Una colección de poemas es como una planta de jitomates. De una semilla nace, luego crece y crece. Los poemas necesitan buena tierra, sol, agua, aire y muchos cuidados y atenciones. Algunos de estos poemas fueron escritos primero en español, otros en inglés y algunos salieron en ambas lenguas casi al mismo tiempo. Los poemas, como los jitomates, se dan en muchas formas y figuras. Y por alguna razón se transforman cada vez que alguien los lee. Ésta es la magia de la poesía.

Comencé a escribir poemas anotando las canciones que mi abuelita nos cantaba. Escribía en la mesa de la cocina, rodeado de nuestras mascotas, a la vez que olía las deliciosas comidas de mi abuela. Para mí, la poesía es vida, familia, comunidad. También pienso que los poemas están de veras incompletos hasta que alguien los lee. Así toman vida y se ponen a bailar en la imaginación. Sí, hazlos tuyos como los hizo suyos la artista Maya Christina Gonzalez. Quiero que sean tan tuyos como son nuestros.

—*Francisco X. Alarcón*

Universal Spiral

there are
no endings

just new
beginnings

Espiral universal

no hay
finales

sólo nuevos
principios.